ESSENTIAL 101 TIPS

BARBECUE

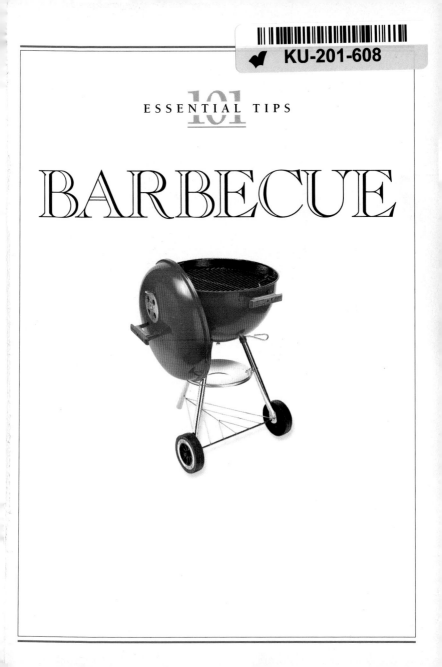

ESSENTIAL TIPS

101

BARBECUE

Marlena Spieler

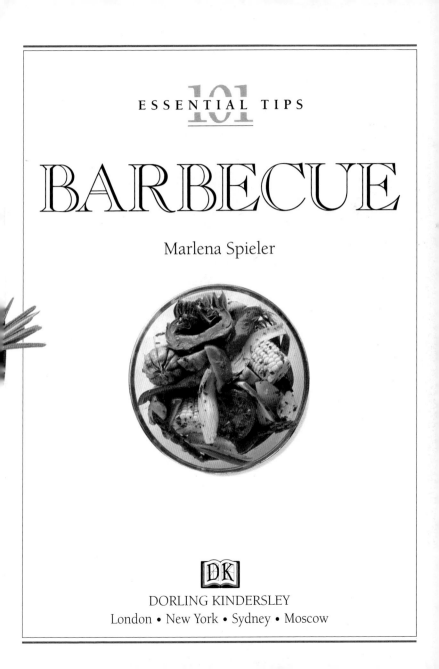

DK

DORLING KINDERSLEY
London • New York • Sydney • Moscow

DK

A DORLING KINDERSLEY BOOK

Editor Bella Pringle
Art Editor Colin Walton
Senior Editor Gillian Roberts
Series Art Editor Alison Donovan
Production Controller Jenny May

**Follow either metric or imperial units throughout a recipe,
never a mixture of the two, since they are not exact equivalents.**

First published in Great Britain in 1998 by
Dorling Kindersley Limited,
9 Henrietta Street, London WC2E 8PS

Visit us on the World Wide Web at http://www.dk.com

A CIP catalogue record for this book is available from the British Library

ISBN 0-7513-0510-3

Text film output by R&B Creative Services Ltd, Great Britain
Reproduced by Colourscan, Singapore
Printed and bound by Graphicom, Italy

ESSENTIAL TIPS

BARBECUE KNOW-HOW

1 WHAT IS A BARBECUE?

A barbecue is a simple method of cooking outdoors. Meat, fish, and vegetables are cooked on a grate or grill over an open fire and quickly absorb the aroma of the smoke, which gives the food its distinct flavour.

◁ BEEF KEBABS (TIP 81)

2 WHERE TO PLACE YOUR BARBECUE

For safety, always place a stand-up barbecue on a firm, level surface so that, once lit, it will not be able to topple over. Place portable models on the ground or on a heatproof surface, but not on a table. Keep all barbecues well away from garden fences, trees, hedges, dry leaves, or any object that could catch a falling spark from the fire and ignite.

3 DIFFERENT KINDS OF BARBECUE

A sophisticated range of barbecues is available. The following review should help you decide which one suits your needs, depending on the number of people you cater for and the kind of food you enjoy cooking.

OPEN-TOP MODELS
If you tend to cook meat that needs quick searing over a high heat, these models are ideal; the coals burn hotter due to their exposure to air.

Open-top models left outdoors may fill with water: choose rust resistant ones

8

Packed up ready to travel

◁ **PORTABLE**
This is just right for small outdoor areas, for example a balcony, and it can be neatly stowed away.

KETTLE BARBECUE ▷
Ideal for cooking whole legs of meat and chicken: the domed lid limits the supply of air to the fire so that the food cooks slowly and with control. The lid also keeps the smoke inside, increasing the flavour of the food.

Fold-out legs hold hot pan base above ground level

Rounded pan and lid reflect heat, providing an even cooking temperature

DISPOSABLE TRAY ▷
For the occasional cook-out, this disposable tray is inexpensive and portable. The foil pan comes pre-packed with fuel.

△ **GAS BARBECUE**
No mess or fuss with this model, fuelled by butane gas. The barbecue taste comes from lava rock, not charcoal or wood.

4 BARBECUE LIGHTING MATERIALS

Achieving a good fire is the key to a successful barbecue. However, it is often in these early stages that many barbecue users have the most problems. Featured here is a range of lighting materials designed to light coals quickly without giving off fumes that may taint the food. There's also a survey of charcoal and wood fuels available, and help in assessing which may suit your cooking needs; the burning time and heat produced can vary, and some have scented smoke.

LIGHTING MATERIALS
You can light the fire in a number of ways. Firelighters and lighter fluid designed for barbecue use work well. But if you want to have coals hot enough for cooking right away, without using chemicals, place an electric heating element under the coals until they ignite (Tip 9), or pack the coals into a fire chimney and light with newspaper (Tip 10).

△ BARBECUE
FIRELIGHTERS

△ LONG
SAFETY MATCHES

△ NEWSPAPER

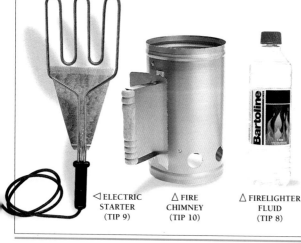

◁ ELECTRIC
STARTER
(TIP 9)

△ FIRE
CHIMNEY
(TIP 10)

△ FIRELIGHTER
FLUID
(TIP 8)

CAUTION!
Use firelighter fluid only before the fire has been lit, and then put it away. Always light the fire with long matches so that you can stand well back. Never squirt petrol or other lighter fluid directly onto the fire since it can flare up, engulfing you in flames.

10

BARBECUE FUELS
Charcoal and wood are the most commonly sold barbecue fuels. To help you to make an informed choice, their properties are outlined below.

▷ **Lump charcoal** is made from whole pieces of wood, with no filler. It burns hotter and cleaner than briquettes.

◁ **Briquettes** contain sawdust, coal, and sand, bound together with a petroleum-based substance. Once lit, they can burn longer than lump charcoal.

▷ **Mesquite charcoal** has a woody scent and burns cleanly.

◁ **Wood fires** are difficult to start but then burn quicker than charcoal or briquettes. Fruit wood such as apple has scented smoke.

5 PREPARING THE FIRE

Food is barbecued directly (placed straight on the grill over the heat of the coals) or indirectly (placed on the grill with a drip pan in the fuel bed beneath). The cooking method determines how you prepare the fire.

△ **DIRECT COOKING**
Arrange the coals in a heap, two layers deep if you intend to cook for more than 45–60 minutes, or in just a single layer if you plan to cook a few items quickly.

△ **INDIRECT COOKING**
Place a foil drip pan in the centre of the fuel bed. Arrange a heap of coals around the edges of the pan, making sure that they are stacked no higher than its sides.

6 USING KINDLING

The best technique for lighting the barbecue with just kindling is to tear off sheets of newspaper, roll them into tight tubes, and then twist them at both ends. Place the newspaper twists in the bottom of the fuel grate, and lay dry twigs or sticks on top. Over this, arrange the coals in a mound leaving air spaces between them. Light the newspaper and add more charcoal, piece by piece, as the fire grows.

For safety, use a long match to light paper, and stand well back

7 USING FIRELIGHTERS

Choose firelighter cubes designed for barbecue use. Then, wearing rubber gloves, arrange the charcoal pieces into a pyramid on the grate. Break one or two firelighters in half and place the pieces between the coals. Light the firelighters using a long safety match, so that you can stand well back. They will burn fiercely for a few minutes, allowing time for the charcoal to ignite.

Arrange lumps of charcoal in a pyramid

Take care: firelighters may flare up

8 USING FIRELIGHTER FLUID

Wearing protective gloves, heap the coals into a pyramid and pour a liberal sprinkling of firelighter fluid over them. Leave the fluid to soak in for a couple of minutes. Put the fluid away in a safe place before lighting the coals, using a taper so that you can stand at arm's length. Once lit, allow the fluid to burn off before cooking, or it may taint the food with a chemical taste.

9 USING AN ELECTRIC STARTER

Arrange the fuel in a small heap at the centre of the grate. Plug in the electric starter to the nearest power point (you may need to use an extension lead). Scoop up the coals in the grate onto the "hand-shaped" heating element. In 1–2 minutes, the electric starter will glow red hot, and the coals will ignite. Unplug the starter and remove it to a safe place so it has time to cool down.

Do not use once the fire is lit

Leave coals to absorb fluid

Once lit, spread coals over grate

Take care when lifting out hot element

10 Using a fire chimney

Coals are packed into the tall metal cylinder, which is separated by a perforated base from the lighting area below (*Tip 4*). The intense heat of the fire is funnelled into the chimney and sets the coals ablaze.

Glowing red-hot coals are ready to use

1 △ Pack the base of the cylinder with newspaper and then place it on the grate for safety. Fill the top section with 40–60 coals. Light the newspaper.

2 △ Within 5–10 minutes, some of the coals will be glowing red. When all are alight, put on a fireproof glove. Carefully pick up the fire chimney by its wooden handle with your gloved hand and gently tip the hot coals into the grate. Use tongs to spread them out; then, you are ready to cook.

11 When can you start cooking?

Many kinds of fuel can take about 45 minutes to burn down to the even heat required for cooking, but some coals such as lumpwood charcoal, which has few impurities, are ready for cooking in about 15 minutes. As a general rule, follow the guidelines on the packaging, and if flames are still licking the coals, the fire is not yet ready for use. Also, different kinds of food need to be cooked over different coal heats. For example, lean meats are best seared over red-hot coals, while larger cuts are best cooked over a slower fire to avoid charring.

12 SCENTING THE SMOKE

The flavour of barbecued foods can be further enhanced by adding natural flavourings such as herbs, cracked nuts, or cinnamon to the charcoal just before cooking. You can also buy manufactured wood chips that increase the flavour of food.

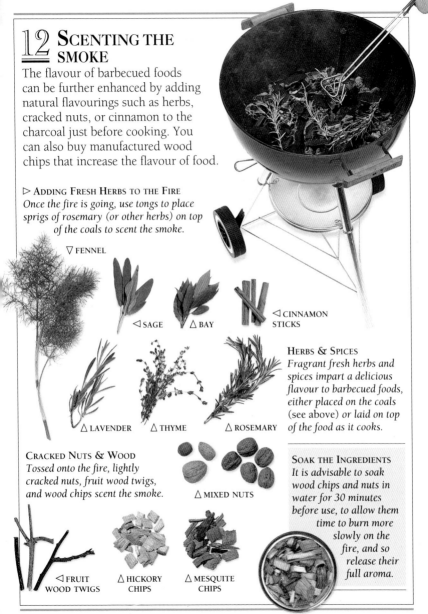

▷ **ADDING FRESH HERBS TO THE FIRE**
Once the fire is going, use tongs to place sprigs of rosemary (or other herbs) on top of the coals to scent the smoke.

▽ FENNEL

◁ SAGE   △ BAY   ◁ CINNAMON STICKS

△ LAVENDER   △ THYME   △ ROSEMARY

HERBS & SPICES
Fragrant fresh herbs and spices impart a delicious flavour to barbecued foods, either placed on the coals (see above) or laid on top of the food as it cooks.

CRACKED NUTS & WOOD
Tossed onto the fire, lightly cracked nuts, fruit wood twigs, and wood chips scent the smoke.

△ MIXED NUTS

◁ FRUIT WOOD TWIGS   △ HICKORY CHIPS   △ MESQUITE CHIPS

SOAK THE INGREDIENTS
It is advisable to soak wood chips and nuts in water for 30 minutes before use, to allow them time to burn more slowly on the fire, and so release their full aroma.

13 USING RED-HOT COALS

At this temperature, food cooks quickly and can burn on the outside while staying raw inside. Sear meat cuts over hot coals to seal in the flavour, or cook lean cuts, such as fish fillets, which will cook right through.

Coals have light dusting of white ash

Coals are glowing red: flames have subsided

◁ GLOWING RED
The coals are now heated thoroughly and reach their top temperature.

Lamb steaks are best seared over hot coals (Tip 79).

14 USING MEDIUM-HOT COALS

This temperature suits most foods since pieces of meat, fish, poultry, and vegetables cook best over moderate heat. If food starts to burn, move it to the outer edges of the grill, which are usually cooler.

Thicker layer of white ash now covers coals

Intense red heat has begun to subside

◁ LAYER OF ASH
The coals start to burn down and reach a moderate temperature.

Fish steaks are cooked over a moderate heat (Tip 63).

15 USING COOL COALS

Once the coals have died down, vegetables and fruit can be warmed on the grill with just a light charring of their skin, or cooked in among the coals. Whole chicken and large cuts of meat also taste good when cooked over a cool fire for 1–2 hours but, for best results, a whole chicken should be cooked on a covered barbecue (*Tip 17*).

Coals no longer show any red

Thick layer of ash covers coals

◁ **DYING DOWN**
The coals have burned down but are still very warm.

Potatoes *can be left to cook in a mound of slow coals for 1–2 hours (Tip 46).*

Sour cream *with chives makes a mouth-watering accompaniment to the potatoes.*

▷ **TESTING THE HEAT**
When the barbecue starts to slow down, you should be able to hold your hand over the grill for about 8 seconds. If you have to pull it away before then, it is still much too hot for slow cooking.

Shallots and cherry tomatoes *can be warmed through as the barbecue cools (Tips 47 & 48).*

17

16 OPEN-TOP BARBECUING

Barbecuing food on an open grill requires constant vigilance: the fire burns hot since air gets to it. It is easy to burn foods on the outside (especially meats), since hot fat dripping onto the coals causes flare-ups. Foods such as hamburgers cook well in these conditions, since the heat chars the food on the outside, sealing in its juices. For foods that need to be cooked right through, the secret is to move the food to the cooler edges of the grill, or to wait for the heat to die down.

Keep people away from open fire

Prawns cook in minutes over medium-hot to hot coals (Tip 59)

Burgers taste superb chargrilled on an open fire (Tip 76).

Lean pork medallions need searing at high temperatures on an open grill (Tip 83).

17 COVERED BARBECUING

Barbecuing food with the cover pulled down will give you more control if you want to cook food slowly and evenly. This works particularly well for large joints of meat and whole fish since the cover reflects heat onto all surfaces of the barbecue and the food cooks on both sides without having to be turned over. Also, food cooking on a covered barbecue will not need to be moved away from hot spots on the grill: you can control the intensity of the heat by opening or closing the air vents in the cover and base of the pan.

Lid and pan contain vents to control draught

Heat from coal is reflected off cover

Chicken pieces cook more evenly under a cover (Tip 67).

▽ **ADJUSTING THE VENTS**
Always wear a heatproof glove before opening or closing the cover vent: the metal is usually very hot and may burn your fingers.

Ribs are more tender the slower they cook (Tip 75).

19

18 USING A DRIP PAN

When cooking a large cut of meat or a whole chicken or other poultry on a covered barbecue, it is a good idea to place a drip pan on the grate below the grill pan to collect the juices for making gravy (*Tip 5*). Before you begin, half fill the drip pan with water, stock, or wine to help prevent the meat from drying out while it is cooking. At 30 minute intervals, lift the cover of the barbecue and check that the liquid in the drip tray has not evaporated; top it up if necessary. Skim the fat off any gravy in the pan before serving it with the meat.

19 SEARING MEAT

A clever way to prevent quick-cooking meat from drying out is to cook it rapidly on both sides to seal in the juices. Finish cooking the meat at the cooler outer edges of the grill.

1 ▷ Using a long-handled basting brush, simply oil the grill rack with vegetable oil so that the meat can be turned without sticking to the metal.

2 △ Using long-handled tongs, place the meat on the centre of the grill – the hottest part – and cook for 1–2 minutes on each side to sear it.

3 △ Remove the seared meat to the cooler edge of the grill and continue cooking for 4–5 minutes a side for rare and up to 10 minutes for well done.

20 BARBECUE TOOLS

Buy long-handled tools, preferably with wood rather than metal handles, for putting food on and taking it off the hot grill. An apron protects your clothes, and fireproof gloves allow you to pick up food cooking on metal skewers, and adjust the barbecue air vents. A hinged basket for cooking fragile fillets of fish is also wise: it will save you the frustration of food slipping through the grill into the fire.

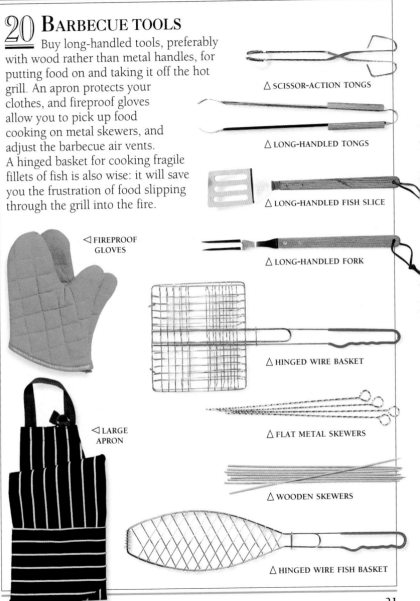

△ SCISSOR-ACTION TONGS

△ LONG-HANDLED TONGS

△ LONG-HANDLED FISH SLICE

◁ FIREPROOF GLOVES

△ LONG-HANDLED FORK

△ HINGED WIRE BASKET

◁ LARGE APRON

△ FLAT METAL SKEWERS

△ WOODEN SKEWERS

△ HINGED WIRE FISH BASKET

21 HOW TO STOKE UP THE FIRE

If the barbecue appears to be dying down and you want to revive it, simply remove the grill and, using long-handled tongs, pick up the coals in turn and tap off the ash until they start to glow again. If the barbecue has air vents, open them wide (wearing gloves if they are still hot) and the draught will fan the fire. Before you resume cooking, heap the coals together.

Tap coals against pan to remove ash

22 COOLING DOWN THE FIRE

If the fire is producing too much heat for your cooking needs and you want to slow it down, first close any vents that are wide open to the half-open position, wearing fireproof gloves. If the barbecue has a cover, put it on. If this doesn't work, try spreading out the coals around the grate to create a less intense bed of heat, using long-handled tongs for safety.

Spread out coals to disperse their heat

23 SHUTTING DOWN THE BARBECUE

When you have finished cooking, dampen down the fire to encourage it to go out of its own accord while you are eating. The hints below outline how to deal with an open-top barbecue, and one with a cover and air vents.

▷ **SPRAY THE COALS WITH WATER**
If you have cooked on an open fire, spread out the coals and spray them thoroughly with water.

Stand well back from fire

◁ **COVER THE COALS**
Place the cover firmly over the cooking top to quash any flames. If the cover has a vent, close it.

▷ **SHUT OFF THE AIR SUPPLY TO THE FUEL**
Suffocate any flames by closing the air vent on the barbecue cover. Make sure that the vent on the bottom of the pan is closed, or this technique will not work.

24 REUSING OLD CHARCOAL

After cooking is finished and the barbecue has cooled down, sift through the ashes before tipping them away. Reserve any half-burnt pieces of charcoal and store them in a cool, dry place for future use.

When laying out coals on the grate for your next barbecue, combine the saved old coals with a quantity of new ones; the recycled material will take longer to catch alight and will not burn as hot.

25 CLEANING THE GRILL AFTER USE

Oil the cooking surface with vegetable oil (*Tip 19, Step 1*) before use to reduce the amount of food that sticks to the grill rack. Clean the grill as soon as the barbecue is cool enough to touch, rather than

leaving it dirty and allowing food particles to set on it overnight. Use kitchen towels to lift surface grease, and scrape off burnt remains with a small wire brush dipped in a hot solution of washing-up liquid.

REMOVE GREASE WITH KITCHEN TOWELS
Meat, poultry, and fish can leave behind a greasy residue on the grill rack. Remove this with kitchen towels so as not to taint the flavour of other foods you may cook.

SCRUB OFF BURNT FOODS
When foods are basted with glazes or marinades, they can leave behind charred remains. Scrub the grill surface vigorously with a wire brush to remove all traces.

MARINADES & RUBS

26 WHY MARINATE?

Meat, fish, poultry, and vegetables that have been marinated for a few hours before barbecuing will take on a wonderful flavour; but as well as the taste, soaking the food in liquid before cooking will make it less likely to dry out when placed over an open fire. Acidic marinades contain wine, vinegar, mustard, or citrus juice to tenderize the food; oil and paste marinades can be spread over the surface of fish or meat to form a savoury protective crust that seals in juices.

MARINADE INGREDIENTS

27 MEAT, POULTRY, GAME

Whole and jointed pieces of meat, poultry, or game need longer marinating times than fish or vegetables. Place the food in a large glass bowl and pour over the marinade. Toss the meat in the mixture to coat well, and leave to absorb the flavours for up to two hours at room temperature or 48 hours in the refrigerator. Bring the food back to room temperature before cooking.

▷ **MARINATING PORK SPARERIBS**
Brush off any excess marinade before cooking or it will char, and grill the ribs until they are brown with a light crust.

28 FRESH FISH & SHELLFISH

Whole and cut fish and shellfish is best marinated before barbecuing to prevent the flesh from drying out when subjected to the heat of the fire. Depending on the marinade you choose, fish can take on a variety of spicy and exotic flavours. Fish absorbs flavour quickly and need be marinated for only 30 minutes at room temperature, or up to two hours in the refrigerator.

▷ **MARINATING FRESH PRAWNS**
Make sure each prawn is covered by the liquid and, when they have finished marinating, drain off the juices before placing the prawns on the grill.

29 FRESH VEGETABLES

Like fish, most vegetables are improved with a light marinade. They need be steeped in liquid only for about 10–30 minutes at room temperature, or up to 2 hours in the refrigerator, depending on how subtle or strong a flavour you want. However, cakes of tofu – a much denser form of vegetable protein – need time for the marinade to penetrate, and are best left overnight to soak in the refrigerator.

◁ **VEGETABLES IN MARINADE**
Heap the vegetables you have ready for barbecuing in a large glass bowl, and pour over the liquid. Toss them to make sure that they are well coated.

30 VEGETABLE & HERB BRUSHES

If you do not have a long-handled brush but want to coat food cooking on the barbecue with extra marinade, try making an improvised brush out of a stick of celery or a leek, or tie together a few sprigs of rosemary and thyme into a mixed herb brush. As well as making useful tools, they will also add flavour to the food as it cooks.

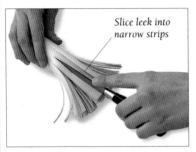

Slice leek into narrow strips

Spread out sprigs to make an effective brush

△ MAKING A LEEK BRUSH
Use a sharp knife to slice up one end of the leek into a series of 5cm (2in) long strands. Spread them out to make a brush.

△ SECURING A HERB BRUSH
Trim five sprigs of herbs into 5cm (2in) lengths and wind string around one end to make a "handle". Tie the string securely.

31 BASIC WINE MARINADE

For 1kg (2lb) meat, poultry, or fish

Ingredients
4 tbsp olive oil
4 tbsp red or white wine
2 shallots, finely chopped or 1 onion, grated
2 garlic cloves, finely chopped (optional)
1 tbsp chopped fresh herbs
salt and black pepper

USES
As a rule, use red wine with red meat and white with chicken or fish.

1 Combine all the ingredients in a glass bowl. Cover with clingfilm if you are not using the marinade at once, and store chilled for 2–3 days.
2 Pour the marinade over the meat or fish of your choice, and toss to coat the food well. Steep for the recommended time (*Tips 27 & 28*) before cooking on the grill for the specified recipe time.

32 LEMON-HERB MARINADE

For 1kg (2lb) chicken, pork or fish, or 750g (1½lb) vegetables

Ingredients

3 garlic cloves, finely chopped
1 lemon, thinly sliced
juice of 1 lemon
3 tbsp olive oil
30g (1oz) mixed fresh parsley, oregano,
sage and rosemary, finely chopped
1 tsp fennel seeds
coarsely ground salt and black pepper

GETTING AHEAD

Prepare the marinade in advance:
it will keep for up to 2 days in
the refrigerator.

1 Mix together all the marinade
ingredients in a large glass dish.
2 Add the food; coat well. Leave
to marinate
(*Tips 27, 28,
& 29*)
before
cooking.

33 SWEET-SPICY MUSTARD MARINADE

For 750g (1½lb) meat or fish

Ingredients

60g (2oz) apricot jam or marmalade
1 tbsp Dijon mustard
30g (1oz) honey
1 tbsp brown sugar
1 tbsp cider vinegar
1 tbsp sesame oil

USES

Marvellous for marinating chicken
wings, prawns, or lamb chops; or use
as a glaze to brush onto the food
just before cooking.

1 Mix together all the ingredients
in a large glass dish.
2 Add the pieces of meat, chicken,
or fish. Leave to marinate for the
suggested time (*Tips 27 & 28*).
3 Cook quickly on a hot grill since
the sugar chars with long cooking.

34 SPICY MEXICAN MARINADE
For 1kg (2lb) fish

Ingredients
3 garlic cloves, finely chopped
1 tbsp chilli powder, lightly toasted
and mixed to a paste with water
1 tbsp paprika
1 tsp ground cumin
½ tsp dried oregano
2 tbsp beer or tequila
juice of 1 orange and 1 lime,
or 3 tbsp pineapple juice
2 tbsp olive oil
2 tbsp chopped fresh coriander
coarsely ground salt, to taste

GETTING AHEAD
Prepare in advance; it will keep for
2–3 days in the refrigerator.

Ingredients
4 tbsp cooked annatto seeds, plus
2 tbsp of the cooking water
2 garlic cloves, finely chopped
½ tsp coarse salt
Spicy Mexican marinade (see above)
½ tsp ground cinnamon
½ tsp ground cloves

USES
Delicious as a marinade for
swordfish steaks or snapper.

1 Combine the ingredients in a
glass dish to form a spicy red paste.
2 Add the food, turn to coat, and
leave to marinate for the suggested
time (*Tip 28*) before cooking.

**VARIATION: ANNATTO &
CHILLI MARINADE**
1 Purée the cooked
annatto seeds and
their cooking water
with the garlic and salt, then
mix with the spicy Mexican
marinade, adding the ground
cinnamon and cloves.
2 Rub the annatto mixture on both
sides of the fish.
3 Place the fish in a glass dish and
leave to marinate at room
temperature for 30–60
minutes, or in the
refrigerator for up
to 3 hours, before
cooking on the grill.

35 TERIYAKI MARINADE

For 1kg (2lb) meat, poultry, or fish

Ingredients
4 tbsp soy sauce
4 tbsp sesame oil
4 tbsp rice wine or dry sherry
2 tbsp sugar
2 spring onions, thinly sliced
2 garlic cloves, chopped
1 tsp grated ginger root

GETTING AHEAD
Prepare this Japanese-style marinade
in advance: it will keep for
2–3 days in the refrigerator.

1 Combine all the ingredients in
a glass dish, and add the food.
2 Turn the food to coat well and
leave to marinate
for the correct
time (*Tips
27 & 28*)
before
cooking.

36 HOISIN MARINADE

For 750g (1½lb) pork chops, duck breasts, or chicken thighs

Ingredients
250ml (8fl oz) hoisin sauce
2–3 tbsp rice vinegar
2 tbsp soy sauce
5 garlic cloves, finely chopped
pinch of five-spice powder
1 tbsp sugar
2 tbsp sesame oil
dash of Tabasco

GETTING AHEAD
Prepare the marinade 2 days
before your barbecue. Cover it
with clingfilm and refrigerate.

1 Combine the ingredients in a
glass bowl and add the food.
2 Turn the food to coat well and
leave to absorb the flavours for the
recommended time (*Tip 27*).
3 Remove the food, and use this
Chinese sauce as a
cooking glaze
(*Tip 42*).

37 INDONESIAN MARINADE

For 1.75kg (3½lb) chicken pieces

Ingredients
5–7 garlic cloves, finely chopped
4 spring onions or 5 shallots, chopped
4 tbsp molasses sugar
grated zest and juice of 2 lemons
2–3 green jalapeño chillies, finely chopped
90ml (3fl oz) soy sauce
½ tsp turmeric
1 tbsp ground coriander
3 tbsp finely chopped ginger root
100g (3½oz) peanuts, ground or finely chopped

GETTING AHEAD
Prepare the marinade 2 days in advance of your barbecue. Cover it and store in the refrigerator.

1 Mix the ingredients in a glass dish and add the chicken pieces.
2 Turn the food to coat well and leave for 3–4 hours at room temperature, or up to 48 hours in the refrigerator for a fuller flavour.

38 TIKKA MASALA MARINADE

For 1kg (2lb) chicken pieces or 285g (9oz) firm tofu

Ingredients
2 garlic cloves, finely chopped
1 tsp chopped ginger root
2 tbsp natural yoghurt
pinch of cayenne pepper
2–3 tsp cumin seeds
pinch of turmeric
1 tbsp tandoori or tikka paste
2 tbsp chopped fresh coriander

USES
This really livens up bland foods such as tofu. The marinade will keep for up to 2 days if stored in the refrigerator.

1 Mix the ingredients together well in a large glass dish.
2 Add the chicken or tofu and turn to coat well. Leave to marinate for the suggested time (*Tips 27 & 29*).

39 USING A DRY RUB

If you do not have time to marinate food overnight, apply a dry mixture of herbs and spices to meat, poultry, or fish about 30 minutes before cooking. Although dry rubs contain no oil to moisten or tenderize the food, the flavour will permeate the flesh. Cuts of meat are easily coated in dry rub, but other foods need help: add a splash of wine or vegetable oil to emulsify the rub and help it stick.

RUBBING SPICES INTO MEAT
Spread a layer of the mixture on a plate and lay the cut of meat on top. Press down on the meat with your fingertips to help the mix to stick. Turn the meat and repeat.

EMULSIFYING THE RUB
To help the herb and spice mixture adhere to drier foods, mix a tablespoon of wine or oil with the spices and herbs to form a smooth paste. Brush over the food.

40 CAJUN SPICE RUB

For 1kg (2lb) meat, fish, or poultry

Ingredients
2 tbsp paprika
1 tbsp ground cumin
1 tbsp dried thyme
1 tbsp onion granules
1 tbsp garlic granules
1tbsp dried oregano
1 tsp black pepper
1 tsp cayenne pepper

1 Place all the ingredients in a bowl and mix.
2 Sprinkle a layer of the mixture on a clean, flat surface.
3 Coat the meat, fish, or poultry on both sides. Leave for 30 minutes to absorb the flavour before barbecuing.

41 WHAT ARE PASTES & GLAZES?

Pastes and glazes are brushed over meat, fish, poultry, or vegetables before, during, and towards the end of cooking to flavour the food. They form a surface coating of flavour rather than being fully absorbed. Pastes are usually made from hot and spicy ingredients, mixed with oil or wine, while glazes use chutneys and jams combined with mustard and sugar to make a sweet caramelized topping. This works particularly well with chicken pieces and other small cuts of meat.

LEEK BRUSH

LONG-HANDLED BASTING BRUSH

42 COOKING GLAZED FOODS

Glazing barbecued foods is one of the easiest ways to liven up a simple piece of meat or poultry. Glazes can be thrown together at a moment's notice from a mixture of storecupboard basics including mustard, sugar, and chutney. The secret of success is patience; glaze the food only when it is nearly cooked, or the sugar will burn.

1 For chicken pieces, first sear on both sides over hot coals, then cook over medium-hot coals for about 20 minutes until the skin is a crisp, golden brown and ready to be glazed before eating.

2 Taking care not to burn yourself on the hot coals, brush a thick layer of glaze over the chicken pieces. Allow it to grill for 2–3 minutes, until it starts to go sticky and becomes slightly charred.

43 MANGO-MUSTARD GLAZE

For a 2kg (4lb) duck, or 750g (1½lb) chops or kebabs

Ingredients

2½ tbsp mango chutney
1½ tbsp Dijon mustard
1½ tbsp marmalade or apricot jam
several drops of Tabasco
or other hot sauce

GETTING AHEAD
Prepare the glaze in advance:
it will keep for up to 2 weeks
in the refrigerator.

1 Mix all the ingredients together in a glass bowl and reserve.
2 When the food is almost cooked, brush on the glaze and continue cooking until the glaze is sticky and just charred.

44 MEXICAN CHILLI PASTE

For 1.75g (3½lb) chicken

Ingredients

grated zest and juice of 1 orange,
1 lime, and 1 lemon
5 garlic cloves, finely crushed
3 tbsp mild chilli powder
1 tbsp paprika
1 tsp ground cumin
½ tsp dried oregano
¼ tsp ground cinnamon
1 tbsp olive oil
1 tsp salt
½ green chilli, chopped, or more to taste

GETTING AHEAD
Prepare the paste in advance: it will keep for 2–3 days in the refrigerator.

1 Mix ½ teaspoon of each fruit zest and all the juices with the other ingredients, adding more spices if you want an even hotter flavour.
2 Before using, leave the paste to thicken at room temperature for 30 minutes.

CHARGRILLED VEGETABLES

45 PARBOILING VEGETABLES

Most vegetables will cook easily on the barbecue from raw, but some tougher vegetables such as artichokes, potatoes, and whole garlic bulbs need parboiling first to soften them. Plunge them into boiling water for 8–10 minutes (5–8 minutes for garlic), then drain.

46 FIRE-BAKED POTATOES

Serves 4 as an appetizer

Ingredients

4 medium-large baking potatoes, washed but unpeeled
vegetable oil, for brushing
olives, salad leaves, and sour cream with chives and shallots, to serve

1 Light the coals well before cooking or preheat a gas barbecue.
2 Prick the potatoes once or twice with a metal skewer so that they won't burst during cooking, then brush the skins with a little oil.
3 Put the potatoes on the grill over medium-cool coals and leave, preferably covered, for 40–60 minutes, turning occasionally to make sure that they cook evenly. Alternatively, place them in a mound of slow coals and leave for 1–2 hours, until they are soft inside when tested with a skewer.
4 Cut into wedges and serve hot with olives, a green salad, and sour cream mixed with finely chopped chives and shallots.

47 FIRE-COOKED SHALLOTS

Serves 4 as a side dish

Ingredients
16 large shallots, unpeeled
3 tbsp olive oil
salt and black pepper

1 Light the barbecue coals well in advance so that they are medium-cool for cooking or preheat a gas barbecue. Soak 4 wooden skewers in cold water for 30 minutes to prevent them from burning when placed on the grill.
2 Meanwhile, put the shallots in boiling water and blanch them for 2–3 minutes to remove their brown outer skins. Rinse well in cold water, drain again and their skins should come away.
3 Thread the shallots onto the prepared skewers, allowing 4 per skewer, and brush both sides with olive oil. Cook the shallots on the grill over a medium-cool fire for about 10–15 minutes, turning occasionally but allowing them to char lightly on the outside.
4 Remove the shallots from the skewers, season with salt and pepper, and serve immediately.

48 FIRE-ROASTED CHERRY TOMATOES

Serves 4 as a side dish

Ingredients
40 cherry tomatoes
salt, 2 tbsp olive oil, and
2–3 garlic cloves, finely chopped
herb-flavoured butter (Tips 86–90),
to serve (optional)

1 Light the barbecue in advance so that the coals are medium-hot for cooking or preheat a gas barbecue. Soak 8 wooden skewers in cold water for 30 minutes.
2 Carefully thread 5 of the cherry tomatoes onto each skewer.
3 Place the filled skewers on the grill and roast over medium-hot coals (covered if possible to control the heat) for about 5–8 minutes or until the tomato skins are just starting to split and the tomatoes are heated through.
4 Serve the fire-roasted tomatoes as soon as they are ready.
5 Remove them from the skewers onto a serving platter or side plates with care, since they will be very soft. Sprinkle with salt, olive oil, and chopped garlic; or dab with a few flecks of herb-flavoured butter.

49 CLASSIC CHARGRILLED VEGETABLES

Serves 4–6 as a side dish or 2–3 as a main course

Ingredients

*2 medium-sized artichokes,
halved and chokes removed*
4 garlic bulbs
8 large tomatoes, halved
2 fennel bulbs, halved or quartered
250g (8oz) asparagus, ends trimmed
4 spring onions, trimmed
2 courgettes, sliced lengthways
*2 sweetcorn, cut into
bite-sized lengths*
8 baby pattypan squash, halved
*1 each green, red, and yellow peppers,
cored, deseeded, and cut into
thick strips or quarters*
*2–3 tbsp chopped mixed fresh herbs,
such as basil, parsley, oregano, rosemary,
thyme, savory, or marjoram*
Garlic Marinade
175ml (6fl oz) olive oil
4 tbsp lemon juice or white wine vinegar
salt and black pepper
4–6 garlic cloves, finely chopped
*1–2 tbsp fresh chopped rosemary or
1 tsp dried herbs, such as
herbes de Provence*

1 Parboil the artichoke halves for 8–10 minutes in boiling water, drain, and place in a shallow dish.
2 Blanch the garlic bulbs in boiling water for 5–8 minutes, then drain.
3 Make the garlic marinade: place the olive oil, lemon juice, seasoning, garlic, and herbs in a bowl and mix well. Spoon about 4 tablespoons of the marinade over the parboiled artichoke halves.
4 Place the garlic and other chopped fresh vegetables in a large bowl and pour over the marinade. Toss the vegetables in the liquid and leave for 30 minutes at room temperature.
5 Light the barbecue shortly before cooking or preheat a gas barbecue.
6 Drain the vegetables, reserving the marinade. Cook the vegetables over hot coals, turning once. As they are ready, remove them to a plate and sprinkle with reserved marinade and fresh herbs.

50 MEDITERRANEAN KEBABS

Serves 4 as a side dish or 2 as a main course

Ingredients

*3–4 courgettes, cut crossways into
1cm (½in) slices*
*1 large yellow pepper, cored, deseeded,
and cut into bite-sized pieces*
16 cherry tomatoes
2 onions, cut into chunks
several sprigs of marjoram or thyme
Mediterranean Marinade
5 garlic cloves, finely chopped
3 tbsp balsamic vinegar
90ml (3fl oz) olive oil
2 tbsp chopped fresh marjoram or thyme
salt and black pepper, to taste

1 Light the barbecue or preheat a gas barbecue. Soak 8 wooden skewers in cold water for 30 minutes to prevent them from burning on the hot grill.
2 Thread each vegetable onto the skewers in turn, followed by a herb sprig, and place in a shallow dish.
3 Mix the marinade ingredients and pour over all the vegetable kebabs. Leave to marinate for 30 minutes at room temperature.
4 Drain the kebabs, reserving the marinade, and cook on the grill over hot coals for about 5 minutes on each side. Serve hot, removed from the skewers and with the reserved marinade poured over.

SOAKING WOODEN SKEWERS
Wooden skewers are ideal for barbecuing meat and vegetable (or even fruit) kebabs because, unlike metal skewers, they do not become too hot to handle when cooking on the grill, and so can be picked up for turning. However, wooden skewers can burn on hot fires. To prevent this, plan ahead and allow the skewers to soak in cold water for 30 minutes before cooking so that they remain damp on the grill and do not burn.

51 GRILLED ASPARAGUS
Serves 4 as a starter or side dish

Ingredients
500–700g (1–1½lb) asparagus tips
White Wine Marinade
125ml (4fl oz) olive oil
2 tbsp lemon juice or balsamic vinegar
2 tbsp dry white wine
1 tbsp wholegrain, Dijon or other French mustard
2 garlic cloves, finely chopped
large pinch of chopped fresh thyme or marjoram
salt and black pepper, to taste

1 Light the barbecue in advance so that it is medium-hot for cooking or preheat a gas barbecue.
2 Mix together all the marinade ingredients in a shallow dish. Add the asparagus tips and coat well, then leave to marinate for 15–20 minutes at room temperature.
3 When the barbecue is ready, drain the asparagus tips and cook for about 3 minutes on each side, depending on the heat of the fire.

52 GRILLED AUBERGINE SLICES
Serves 4 as an appetizer or side dish

Ingredients
1 large or 2 small to medium aubergines, cut crossways into 1cm (½in) slices
olive oil, for basting
2 tbsp red or white wine vinegar, or to taste
½ onion, finely chopped
3–4 tbsp chopped fresh parsley
salt and black pepper, to taste

1 Light the barbecue in advance so that the coals are medium-hot for cooking or preheat a gas barbecue.
2 Brush the aubergine slices with olive oil on both sides. Cook over medium-hot coals until the first side has brown grill marks, then turn and cook the other side.
3 Remove from the heat and dress the slices with a little each of chopped onion, parsley, and seasoning. Allow the slices to cool slightly before serving at room temperature.

USING COOKED SLICES
When you have grilled the slices of aubergine, purée the smoky flesh in a food processor, with a bit of freshly squeezed lemon juice, to make an appetizing dip

53 BRUSCHETTA

Serves 4 as an appetizer

Ingredients

*4 x 2.5cm (1in) thick slices
of country bread,
such as ciabatta
4 garlic cloves, halved
extra-virgin olive oil,
to taste
salt, to taste (optional)
Toppings, to serve
(see below)*

1 Light the barbecue in advance so that the coals are medium-hot for cooking or preheat a gas barbecue.
2 Toast the bread slices on both sides over medium-hot coals until crisp and golden brown.
3 Rub both sides of each slice with the cut garlic. Drizzle with olive oil and serve with one of the following topping suggestions.

**BRUSCHETTA
WITH HERBS**

◁ **TOMATOES & BASIL**
*Top with slices of
fire-roasted cherry
tomatoes (Tip 48)
and garnish with
fresh basil.*

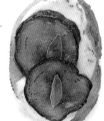

◁ **AUBERGINE SLICES
& MOZZARELLA**
*Layer generous slices
of mozzarella and
chargrilled aubergine
slices on the toasts.*

▷ **SWEET PEPPERS**
*Chargrill yellow
peppers (Tip 49)
and cut them into
fine slivers to make
a simple, colourful,
and delicious topping
for bruschetta.*

▷ **MOZZARELLA & BASIL**
*For a quick, appetizing snack,
arrange two slices of buffalo
mozzarella on warm
bruschetta and just
sprinkle with fresh basil.*

△ **TAPENADE & ROCKET**
*Olive paste (tapenade)
garnished with fresh
rocket leaves is a perfect
foil to the garlicky
toasted bruschetta.*

BARBECUED FISH

54 FISH COOKING TIMES

Being cooked on an open fire enhances all kinds of fresh fish and shellfish. Cooking times, which vary, depend on the thickness of the flesh and whether there is a shell or not.

- **Whole fish or steaks:** Cook over hot coals for 10 minutes per 2.5cm (1in) of thickness. Cook whole fish in a wire basket to keep it intact.
- **Fillets:** Cook for 2–3 minutes a side in a hinged basket (*Tip 55*).
- **Kebabs:** Cook over medium-hot coals for about 5 minutes a side, depending on the heat of the fire.

- **Jumbo prawns:** Place on wooden skewers and then cook over hot coals for 5–10 minutes a side.
- **Clams & mussels:** Cook covered over hot coals. Allow 8–10 minutes for mussels, 10–12 for clams.
- **Lobster & crab:** Allow 10–15 minutes over hot coals, but do not overcook.

55 WAYS TO COOK FISH

Fish is more fragile than meat and poultry, and tends to fall apart quite easily during cooking. When grilling fish on a barbecue, it is important to be able to turn the fish easily without it sticking to the grill and breaking.

Fish pieces can be secured on wooden or metal skewers (*Tip 61*), while fragile fillets are best cooked in a hinged wire basket so that they can be easily turned with the minimum of fuss. Whole fish can be grilled in a specially designed fish-shaped wire basket (*Tip 56*) or wrapped in vine leaves (*Tip 57*).

ENCLOSE FISH FILLETS IN A WIRE BASKET

56 GRILLING LARGER FISH WHOLE

Larger fish such as snapper and sea bass are best cooked in a rigid wire basket to keep the fish whole. Cut 2 or 3 diagonal slashes on both sides of the fish so that the smoky flavour penetrates.

FISH BASKET

57 WRAPPING FISH IN VINE LEAVES

When fish is wrapped in vine leaves for cooking, its flesh stays moist since the fish does not come into direct contact with the fire. The leaves also add a delicious flavour.

Stuff with rolled-up vine leaves and sage

1 ▷ Clean (and, if necessary, descale) the fish. Hold it open and fill the cavity with a stuffing of your choice to enhance the flavour when cooked.

2 △ Spread out 2–3 vine leaves on a clean, dry surface and place the fish in the middle. Leaving the head and tail free, carefully wrap the leaves around the fish, covering up any exposed skin.

3 △ Secure the leaves in place with string tied around the fish at regular intervals. Fasten each piece of string with a knot. Trim the ends of the string, and take the fish to the fire for cooking.

58 CHARGRILLED SARDINES

Serves 4 as a main course

Ingredients

1kg (2lb) whole sardines or
sprats, cleaned only if
larger than
10–12cm (4–5in)
3 garlic cloves, finely
chopped
juice of ½ lemon
2 tbsp Pernod, ouzo, or
other spirit flavoured
with aniseed
3 tbsp olive oil
2 tbsp chopped fresh
parsley
salt and black pepper
lemon wedges, to garnish
raw fennel and red pepper
strips, dressed with
vinaigrette, to serve

1 Place the fish in a large shallow dish and add the garlic, lemon juice, Pernod, olive oil, and half the chopped parsley. Turn to coat the fish well in the liquid, then leave to marinate for 30–60 minutes at room temperature.

2 Light the coals in advance so that they are hot for cooking or preheat a gas barbecue.

3 Drain the sardines, discarding the marinade, and cook the fish quickly over the hot coals for about 3–4 minutes on each side, until they show grill marks on the skin and the flesh is cooked through. (If the fish are grilled on a covered barbecue, they may not need turning.)

4 Season the cooked fish well, then serve hot off the grill, garnished with wedges of fresh lemon and sprinkled with the remaining parsley. Serve with a salad of raw fennel and red peppers.

59 THAI-STYLE PRAWNS

Serves 4 as a starter or 6 as a main course

Ingredients

12 or 24 (starter or main course) raw tiger prawns in their shells, heads removed
1 walnut-sized piece of creamed coconut blended with 4 tbsp water or 4 tbsp unsweetened coconut milk
red chillies, to garnish
Thai Marinade
¼ red pepper, cored, deseeded, and finely chopped
4 garlic cloves, finely chopped
2 tbsp chopped fresh coriander
2 tbsp vinegar
juice of 2 limes
1 stalk lemon grass, finely chopped or grated rind of ¼ lemon
½ tsp turmeric, or to taste
4 tbsp vegetable oil
pinch of ground cumin
1–2 fresh green chillies, finely chopped
½ tsp crushed dried red chillies or red chilli paste
1 tsp sugar, or to taste

1 Light the barbecue in advance so that it is medium-hot or preheat a gas barbecue.
2 Combine all the marinade ingredients in a bowl. Place the tiger prawns in a shallow dish and pour over the marinade. Turn until well coated, then leave for 30 minutes at room temperature.
3 Soak 4 or 8 wooden skewers in cold water for 30 minutes to stop them burning on the grill.
4 Drain the prawns, reserving the marinade. Thread 3 prawns on each skewer, piercing each prawn in two places. Cook over medium-hot coals for about 2–3 minutes on each side, basting once or twice with the marinade, until the prawns are pink and slightly charred.
5 Meanwhile, pour the reserved marinade into a small pan, stir in the coconut liquid, and heat until the sauce thickens (about 5 minutes). To serve, pour the hot sauce over the prawns.

60 FISH FROM THE GREEK ISLANDS

Serves 6–8 as a main course

Ingredients

*2 whole fish, such as
red or grey mullet, red
snapper, or tilapia, about
1kg (2lb) each
juice of 2 lemons
salt and black pepper
125ml (4fl oz) olive oil
6 bay leaves, plus extra
to garnish
1 tsp dried oregano,
crumbled*

1 Light the barbecue in advance so that the coals are hot for cooking.

2 With a sharp knife, score the fish diagonally at 5cm (2in) intervals. Rub the fish inside and out with half the lemon juice, salt and pepper, and 2 tablespoons of the olive oil. Place 3 bay leaves inside each fish and sprinkle both inside and out with the dried oregano.

3 Secure the fish in a wire basket and cook for about 15 minutes on each side over hot coals.

4 Sprinkle the cooked fish with the remaining lemon juice and oil, and garnish with bay leaves.

61 MONKFISH KEBABS

Serves 4–6 as a main course

Ingredients

*750g (1½lb) monkfish
steaks, cut into
about 30 chunks
salt, to taste
2 tbsp olive oil
Aïoli
1 garlic clove, crushed
1 large free-range egg
1 tbsp French mustard
juice of ½ lemon
salt and cayenne pepper,
to taste
200–250ml (7–8fl oz)
olive oil*

TAKE HEED
Aïoli contains
uncooked egg.

1 Light the barbecue in advance so that the coals are hot for cooking.

2 To make aïoli, blend the garlic in a food processor with the whole egg, mustard, lemon juice, salt, and cayenne pepper.

3 Slowly add the olive oil to the mixture, a drop at a time. Once half the oil has been blended in, add the rest in a thin stream. Blend until thickened, then refrigerate.

4 Thread the chunks of monkfish onto skewers. Sprinkle with salt and brush with olive oil. Cook over hot coals for 3–4 minutes on each side. Serve with the aïoli, and Mojo rojo (*Tip 92*).

62 GRILLED SALMON WITH LEEKS

Serves 4 as a main course

Ingredients

8 baby leeks, cleaned and trimmed
4 x 2.5cm (1in) thick salmon steaks,
about 250g (8oz) each
3 tbsp olive oil or melted butter
salt and black pepper

Chive, Lemon, & Watercress Butter
60g (2oz) butter, softened
1 garlic clove, finely chopped
1 shallot, finely chopped
2 tbsp chopped chives
45g (1½oz) watercress, chopped
juice of ½ lemon
salt and black pepper

1 Light the barbecue in advance so that the coals are medium-hot for cooking or preheat a gas barbecue.
2 While you are waiting, make the flavoured butter. Blend the softened butter with the garlic, shallot, chives, and watercress, then stir in the lemon juice and seasoning. Drain off any excess liquid and mould the butter into a log. Wrap in clingfilm and chill in the refrigerator until firm.
3 Blanch the leeks in boiling water for about 2 minutes, then drain, refresh under cold running water, and drain again, to remove their outer layer.
4 Brush the salmon and the leeks with olive oil or melted butter. Season with salt and pepper.
5 Place the fish steaks and leeks directly on the grill and cook for 3–5 minutes on each side, until the salmon is firm and the leeks are just charred.
6 Serve at once, with a slice of the chilled butter on top of each salmon steak.

63 SWORDFISH WITH ANNATTO & CHILLI

Serves 4 as a main course

Ingredients

*Annatto & chilli marinade
and Spicy Mexican
marinade (Tip 34)*
½ tsp crushed stick cinnamon
½ tsp ground cloves
*4 swordfish steaks, about
750g (1½lb) total weight*
*handful of fresh bay leaves,
to scent the barbecue*
*bay leaves and lemon
slices, to garnish*
*diced onion, avocado,
tomatoes, pickled chillies,
and chopped fresh
coriander, to serve*

1 Mix together both marinades, adding the cinnamon and cloves. Rub the mixture on both sides of the fish. Leave for 30 minutes at room temperature or for up to 3 hours in the refrigerator, so that the spicy rub can permeate the flesh of the fish.

2 Light the barbecue and place the bay leaves on the coals to produce fragrant smoke (*Tip 12*).

3 Cook the fish over medium-hot coals for about 5 minutes on each side or until it is golden brown and slightly charred.

4 Mix the onion, avocado, tomatoes, chillies, and coriander. Serve alongside the fish.

64 CAJUN FISH & GOLDEN COURGETTES

Serves 4 as a main course

Ingredients

*4 cod fillets, about
750g (1½lb) total weight*
Cajun spice rub (Tip 40)
*2 yellow courgettes, sliced
into 3mm (⅛in) thick strips*
*Sundried tomato & basil
butter (Tip 88), to serve*
*2 spring onions,
thinly sliced, and 1–2 tbsp
chopped fresh coriander, to
sprinkle on the cooked fish
and courgette strips*

1 Using three quarters of the Cajun spice rub, coat the cod fillets on both sides. Leave the dry rub to flavour the fish for at least 30 minutes at room temperature.

2 Light the barbecue or preheat a gas barbecue.

3 Place the cod fillets in a wire basket so that they do not disintegrate on the grill, and cook over hot coals, allowing 2–3 minutes on each side or until the fillets flake easily.

4 When the fish is half cooked, dust the strips of courgette with the remaining Cajun spice rub and place on the grill. Cook for 2–3 minutes, turning several times, until lightly charred.

BARBECUED POULTRY

65 CHICKEN COOKING TIMES

Use this guide to ensure that your chicken is thoroughly cooked.

- **Pieces:** Sear on both sides over hot coals, then cook on medium-hot coals; dark meat takes 30 minutes; white meat, 15 minutes.
- **Breasts, boned:** Cook quickly over medium-hot coals for about 2–3 minutes a side.
- **Half:** Cook, covered, over medium-hot heat for 30 minutes.
- **Whole:** Cook, covered, over moderate heat (55°C/135°F) for about 1–1½ hours.

CHICKEN
WINGS

- **Chicken wings:** Cook directly over hot or medium-hot coals for about 10 minutes a side.

66 HOW TO TEST IF POULTRY IS DONE

The skin of chicken, turkey, and duck soon turns a crispy golden brown when grilled on a barbecue, so it is difficult to tell whether the meat is properly cooked on the inside. Caution is needed since raw poultry carries salmonella. A good test is to pierce the flesh with a skewer. As you pull it out, check to see that the juices run clear – a sign that the flesh is thoroughly cooked.

PIERCE LEG WITH A SKEWER TO TEST

67 TUSCAN CHICKEN
Serves 4 as a main course

Ingredients

*1.5kg (3lb) whole chicken,
jointed into 8 pieces
1 yellow and 1 red pepper,
cored, deseeded, and
cut into wedges
4 small courgettes, sliced
lengthways
500g (1lb) asparagus,
ends trimmed
black olives, to garnish
Tuscan Marinade
10 garlic cloves,
finely chopped
juice of 3 lemons
2–3 tbsp chopped
fresh rosemary
salt and black pepper
90ml (3fl oz) olive oil
Aïoli (Tip 61), to serve*

1 To make the marinade, combine the garlic, lemon juice, rosemary, a good pinch of salt, some black pepper, and the olive oil in a small bowl. Mix well to blend.

2 Place the chicken pieces in a large shallow dish. Pour two-thirds of the marinade over the chicken. Reserve the rest of the marinade to use with the accompanying vegetables. Leave the chicken to marinate for a minimum of 2 hours (or up to 48 hours) in the refrigerator.

3 Light the barbecue or preheat a gas barbecue.

4 When the coals are medium-hot, arrange the chicken on the grill. Put dark meat on the grill first since it takes longer to cook than white meat (*Tip 65*). Move the pieces around so that they cook evenly. If the barbecue has a cover, use it to create a more even temperature.

5 When the chicken is almost done (check by piercing the flesh with a skewer – *Tip 66*), toss the peppers, courgettes, and asparagus in half the reserved marinade. Arrange the vegetables on the grill and cook for about 2 minutes on each side, basting them with the rest of the marinade.

6 To serve, pile the vegetables around the chicken pieces. Garnish with black olives and serve with aïoli.

TAKE HEED
Aïoli contains uncooked egg. Do not serve it to the elderly, young children, or pregnant women.

68 CHICKEN WINGS SATAY

Serves 4 as a starter

Ingredients

1kg (2lb) chicken wings
6 garlic cloves,
finely chopped
2 tbsp chopped ginger root
90–125g (3–4oz) sugar,
or to taste
4 tbsp dry sherry
or rice wine
125ml (4 fl oz) dark
soy sauce
2 tbsp sesame oil
6 spring onions
Indonesian peanut sauce
(Tip 91), to serve

1 Place the chicken wings, garlic, ginger, sugar, sherry, soy sauce, and sesame oil in a shallow dish. Toss well, then cover and marinate for not less than 3 hours at room temperature.

2 Light the coals in advance, so that they are hot for cooking or preheat a gas barbecue.

3 Grill the chicken wings for about 10 minutes a side, or until browned and crisp. A minute or two before the end of cooking, add the spring onions to the grill. Serve the Indonesian peanut sauce as a dip alongside the chicken wings.

69 STUFFING A CHICKEN BREAST

A simple and quick way to enhance the flavour of chicken breasts to be cooked on the grill is to stuff them with ingredients full of flavour, such as wild mushrooms. These steps show you how.

1 Using a sharp knife, cut a deep lengthways slit into the raw chicken breast to form a large pocket for the stuffing.

2 Open up the pocket in the flesh with the knife, and carefully spoon 3 or 4 teaspoons of the stuffing into the pocket.

3 To prevent stuffing from falling out, fasten the opening by skewering the flesh twice with cocktail sticks.

70 CHICKEN WITH MUSHROOMS
Serves 4 as a main course

Ingredients
6–8 fresh or dried morels
6–8 ceps (porcini) or
6 slices dried ceps
4 boned and skinned
chicken breasts
1 shallot, chopped
2 garlic cloves, finely chopped
2 tbsp olive oil
juice of ¼ lemon
salt and black pepper
Shallot butter (Tip 89) with 1 tbsp
deseeded, chopped fresh red chilli
mixed in, to serve
salad leaves and chives, to garnish

1 If using dried morels and ceps, rehydrate them by soaking them in boiling water for 30 minutes. Then, drain the mushrooms and squeeze out any excess liquid. Coarsely chop the rehydrated or fresh mushrooms and set aside.

2 Light the barbecue or preheat a gas barbecue.

3 Cut a pocket lengthways in each chicken breast, then fill each with a quarter of the chopped mushrooms (*Tip 69*). Arrange the stuffed breasts in a shallow glass dish.

4 Mix together the shallot, garlic, olive oil, lemon juice, salt, and pepper. Pour over the chicken breasts and turn to coat well. Cover and leave to marinate at room temperature for at least 1 hour.

5 Cook the stuffed chicken breasts over hot coals for at least 4 minutes a side, until they are cooked through and the juices run clear when pierced with a skewer (*Tip 66*). Avoid overcooking and serve with slices of Shallot butter (*Tip 89*). Garnish with salad leaves and sprigs of chives.

71 CHICKEN TIKKA KEBABS

Serves 4 as a main course

Ingredients

4 boned, skinned chicken breasts,
about 1kg (2lb) total weight,
cut into bite-sized pieces
juice of 1 lemon
30ml (1oz) butter, melted
Tikka Marinade
150g (5fl oz) natural yoghurt
3 garlic cloves, finely chopped
2 tsp ground coriander
½ tsp turmeric
1½ tsp ground cumin
1½ tbsp paprika
¼ tsp ground ginger
large pinch of cayenne pepper
1 tbsp tamarind paste or mango chutney

1 Arrange the chicken pieces in a shallow dish, pour over the lemon juice, and leave to tenderize for 15–30 minutes.
2 Mix together all the marinade ingredients, pour over the chicken, and turn to coat well. Cover; leave for up to 3 hours at room temperature.
3 Light the barbecue.
4 Thread the chicken onto soaked wooden skewers, and brush with the butter.
5 Cook over hot coals, preferably covered, for about 3 minutes a side.

72 HOW TO SPATCHCOCK POULTRY

The technique described here is used to make a whole chicken or poussin an even thickness so that all parts of the bird will cook at the same rate, preventing thinner parts of the flesh from drying out.

1 Using a strong pair of kitchen scissors, remove the backbone by cutting along one side and then the other.

2 Lay the chicken skin-side down and press down firmly on the bird with the heel of your hand to flatten it out.

3 To hold the chicken flat while it cooks. secure the wings and legs in place with a crisscross of bamboo skewers.

73 SPATCHCOCKED POUSSINS & HERBS

Serves 4 as a main course

Ingredients

60g (2oz) unsalted butter
1½ tbsp aromatic wine vinegar,
such as rosemary or garlic
4 garlic cloves, finely chopped
4 poussins, spatchcocked (Tip 72)
salt and black pepper
2 tsp mixed dried herbs, including thyme,
marjoram, rosemary, fennel, and savory
½ tsp crumbled dried bay leaves
15g (½oz) fresh basil leaves,
torn into pieces
fresh rosemary sprigs, to garnish

1 Light the barbecue coals well in advance or preheat a gas barbecue.
2 Over a low barbecue heat, melt half the butter in a small pan. Add the vinegar and garlic and cook for 1–2 minutes, then set aside.
3 Season the poussins, rubbing in the salt and pepper, then brush the skins with the melted butter and sprinkle with dried herbs.
4 To flavour the flesh, loosen the skin in places along the breast and thighs and stuff with flecks of the unmelted butter and torn basil leaves. Then, make small cuts over the rest of the skin and insert more butter and basil as before. Cover and leave the poussins for 30–60 minutes at room temperature.
5 Barbecue the poussins over medium-hot coals for 20–30 minutes, until golden brown on the outside but still moist inside, turning occasionally. The poussins are cooked if the juices run clear when the thigh is pierced with a skewer (*Tip 66*). Serve garnished with rosemary sprigs.

BARBECUED MEAT

74 HOW LONG TO COOK?

The cooking times described here will help you judge how long to cook small cuts of meat on the barbecue. When cooking large joints, use a meat thermometer to determine the cooking time more accurately.

MEAT THERMOMETER

BEEF COOKING TIMES

- **Hamburgers** Cook over medium-hot coals for 3 minutes on one side. Turn and cook the hamburgers for a further 3 minutes for rare or up to 10 minutes for well done.
- **Steaks** Sear for 1 minute a side, then cook for 4 minutes a side for rare or up to 8 for well done.
- **Beef (or lamb) kebabs** Cook over medium-hot coals for 3–4 minutes a side for rare or up to 6–7 minutes if you like your meat well done.

LAMB COOKING TIMES

- **Lamb chops** For 2.5–3.5cm (1–1½in) thick chops, sear and cook over medium-hot coals for 4–5 minutes a side for rare or up to 8 for well done.

PORK COOKING TIMES

- **Loin or rib chops** For 2.5cm (1in) thick chops, sear both sides, then cook, covered, over medium-hot coals for 6–8 minutes a side.
- **Spareribs** Cook, preferably covered, over medium-hot, indirect heat until tender (1–2 hours for sheet ribs), then directly over the heat to char. Alternatively, precook ribs in foil, then barbecue over hot coals for about 10 minutes a side.
- **Kebabs** Cook either covered or uncovered over medium-hot coals for 5–6 minutes a side (the meat should be cooked right through).

SAUSAGE COOKING TIMES

- **Beef, lamb, pork, or veal** Prick the skins, then cook over medium-hot coals for about 5 minutes a side. Cook pork sausages for an extra 3 minutes a side.

75 ALL-AMERICAN RIBS

Serves 4 as a main course

Ingredients

*1kg (2lb) pork spareribs,
either in a sheet or separated*
*4 leeks, cut into brushes
(Tip 30), for basting*

Down-home Dry Rub
1 tbsp onion granules
1 tbsp salt
1 tsp black pepper
3 tbsp paprika
1 tbsp dry mustard
1 tbsp garlic granules
*1 tbsp crumbled dried
bay leaves*

Lone Star Moppin' Sauce
150ml (¼ pint) cider vinegar
90ml (3fl oz) vegetable oil
*60ml (4 tbsp)
Worcestershire sauce*
*½ tsp Tabasco or other
hot sauce*
1 tbsp paprika
1 tbsp mild chilli powder
1 tsp English mustard powder
*1 tsp crumbled dried
bay leaves*
1 tsp garlic granules
½ tsp celery salt, or to taste
*She-devil barbecue sauce
(Tip 95), for brushing*

1 Mix the dry rub ingredients together in a bowl. Dust the ribs with the mixture, then rub it in well. Leave the ribs for 30 minutes at room temperature to absorb the flavour.
2 Light the barbecue well in advance so that the fire will be medium-cool for cooking or preheat a gas barbecue.
3 To make the mopping sauce, place all the listed ingredients in a mixing bowl and blend together well.
4 Cook the ribs over cool coals. Using a leek brush, baste the spare ribs from time to time on the grill with mopping sauce. If possible, cover the grill: the longer and slower the ribs cook, the more tender the meat will be. If the ribs are in a sheet, allow about 1–2 hours cooking time; 40 minutes if separated.
5 When the ribs are almost done, brush them with She-devil barbecue sauce. Serve at once, offering any remaining sauce separately.

76 CLASSIC HAMBURGERS

Serves 4 as a main course

Ingredients

750g (1½lb) lean minced beef
8 shallots or 1 onion, finely chopped
*3–4 tbsp double cream or extra-thick
single cream*
4 small ice cubes
salt and black pepper
Shredded Lettuce Burger Sauce
125g (4oz) prepared mayonnaise
*3 tbsp French mustard, or a combination
of brown and American yellow mustard*
*½ iceberg lettuce or 1 whole green
lettuce, shredded*
4 shallots, finely chopped
juice of ½ lemon
4 sesame buns
*sliced tomatoes, onions, and pickled
gherkins, to garnish*

1 Light the barbecue in advance so that the coals will be hot or preheat a gas barbecue.

2 Place the minced beef in a large bowl and break it up with a fork. Add the shallots and cream and beat with a wooden spoon until the mixture is well combined.

3 Using clean, wet hands so that the mixture does not stick to them, divide then flatten into patties about 2.5cm (1in) thick. Insert an ice cube into the centre of each patty to keep the meat moist during cooking on the barbecue.

4 Generously season the patties with salt and pepper and place on the barbecue over hot coals. Cook for 3 minutes, then turn to cook the other side. Continue until the meat is done to taste (*Tip 74*).

5 To make the sauce, blend the mayonnaise and mustard together in a bowl. Add the lettuce and shallots, and toss until well combined. Add lemon juice to taste.

6 Split the sesame buns in half and lightly toast them on the barbecue. Serve each burger in a bun, topped with lettuce sauce. Garnish with slices of tomato, raw onion rings, and gherkins.

77 SAUSAGE SELECTION

Serves 4 as a main course

Ingredients

*1kg (2lb) assorted sausages,
such as smoked kielbasa,
Toulouse, chorizo, bratwurst
4 onions, peeled and halved
1 each red, yellow, and green
peppers, halved and deseeded
2 fennel bulbs, quartered
lengthways
2–3 tbsp olive oil
juice of ½ lemon
salt and black pepper
relishes, to serve*

1 Light the barbecue or preheat a gas barbecue.
2 Prick the sausages and cook over medium-hot coals for 5 minutes a side (*Tip 74*).
3 Meanwhile, toss the vegetables in olive oil and lemon juice; season. Place around the cooler edges of the grill; cook until tender.
4 As individual sausages and vegetables are cooked through, remove from the grill and keep warm. Serve with a choice of relishes.

78 MOROCCAN LAMB BROCHETTES

Serves 4 as a main course

Ingredients

*750g (1½lb) boneless lamb
chump chops, cut into
bite-sized pieces
1 onion, finely chopped
5 garlic cloves, finely chopped
2 tsp crumbled dried bay
leaves or herbes de Provence
pinch of dried thyme
2 tsp ground cumin
½ tsp turmeric
juice of 1½ lemons
90ml (3fl oz) olive oil
salt and black pepper
1 tbsp paprika
1 tbsp chopped fresh coriander*

1 Place the lamb pieces in a dish with the onion, garlic, bay leaves, thyme, half the cumin, turmeric, lemon juice, and olive oil. Mix well, then marinate for at least 30 minutes or, if there is time, up to 3 hours at room temperature or overnight in the refrigerator.
2 Light the barbecue.
3 Thread the lamb onto soaked wooden skewers (*Tip 50*), then season to taste. Cook over hot coals until browned on one side, about 5 minutes, then turn and cook the other side for another 5 minutes.
4 Sprinkle with the remaining cumin, and the paprika and coriander, and serve.

79 CUMIN ROAST LAMB

Serves 4 as a main course

Ingredients

4 baby leeks or small
peeled brown onions, or
8 spring onions, trimmed
500g (1lb) pumpkin or
other orange winter
squash, unpeeled and cut
into 5mm (¼in) slices
1 aubergine, cut into
wedges or thick slices
2 tbsp olive oil
juice of ½ lemon
4 lamb steaks, about
175–250g (6–8oz) each
fresh coriander leaves,
to garnish
Cumin Paste
2 tbsp cumin seeds
2 tbsp ground cumin
6 garlic cloves, crushed
1 tsp salt
4 tbsp olive oil
2 tbsp chopped fresh
coriander or parsley
juice of 1 lemon

1 Place all the cumin paste ingredients in a bowl and mix together.

2 Blanch the leeks for 1–2 minutes in boiling water, then drain. Place in a shallow dish with the pumpkin and aubergine.

3 Drizzle the vegetables with olive oil and lemon juice, then add 1–2 tablespoons of the cumin paste and toss the vegetables to coat them.

4 Place the lamb steaks in a shallow dish and add the remaining cumin paste, turning to coat well on all sides. Cover and leave the lamb and vegetables to marinate for at least 30 minutes at room temperature.

5 Light the barbecue so that the coals are hot for cooking or preheat a gas barbecue.

6 Place the meat and vegetables on the grill over hot coals. Turn everything once or twice while cooking, so that the lamb steaks are browned on the outside but still pink inside, and the vegetables are tender, with grill marks.

7 Garnish with fresh coriander leaves.

TO SERVE
Accompany this dish
with Middle Eastern
spiced pilaff (Tip 101)
and Cucumber-yoghurt
raita (Tip 94), if liked.

80 FAJITAS

Serves 4 as a main course

Ingredients

250g (8oz) skirt steak or
other tender beef steak,
in one piece
Mexican chilli paste
(Tip 44)
4 tbsp tequila
1 chicken breast, boned
but not skinned
2 chorizo sausages,
poached (optional)
4 small onions, unpeeled,
halved lengthways
2 ripe plantains, peeled,
halved lengthways
12 flour tortillas
2 tbsp sour cream
1 red chilli, finely chopped
sliced limes, coriander, and
shredded lettuce, to garnish

1 Spread about half of the Mexican chilli paste over the beef, and leave to stand at room temperature for 10 minutes to absorb some of the flavour. Sprinkle over 2 tablespoons of tequila, cover the meat with clingfilm, and place in the refrigerator to marinate overnight.
2 Spread the rest of the chilli paste over the chicken breast, sprinkle with the remaining tequila, and refrigerate for at least 1–2 hours.
3 Light the barbecue.
4 Cook the beef over hot coals for 8–10 minutes, turning once, until it is cooked on the outside but still rare inside, or to taste (*Tip 74*).
5 When the beef is half cooked, place the whole chicken breast on the grill and cook for about 4 minutes on each side, or until the juices run clear when pierced with a skewer (*Tip 66*). Add the poached sausages, if using, onions, and plantains, and grill for 2–3 minutes on each side.
6 Sprinkle each tortilla with a little cold water to keep it moist, then grill for 30 seconds on each side. Keep warm in a clean tea towel.
7 Remove the onions and plantains from the grill and place them on a serving platter. Slice the beef and chicken into thin strips (cut up the sausages). Arrange all the meat (and sausages) on the platter; sprinkle with the chopped chilli.
8 Serve the meat (and sausages) wrapped up in the tortillas, together with accompaniments such as sour cream, Guacamole (*Tip 97*), Salsa (*Tip 98*), and Refried beans (*Tip 99*). Garnish each serving with sliced limes, coriander leaves, and shredded lettuce.

81 BEEF SHISH KEBAB

Serves 4 as a main course

Ingredients

750g (1½lb) sirloin or other prime cut of beef, cut into bite-sized cubes
3–5 garlic cloves, finely chopped
1 small onion, chopped
10 black peppercorns, coarsely ground
250ml (8 fl oz) red wine
handful of fresh bay leaves
3 small onions, peeled and cut into wedges
3 green peppers, halved, deseeded, and cut into wedges
125ml (4 fl oz) sunflower oil
salt and black pepper

1 Place the cubed beef in a glass dish with the garlic, onion, peppercorns, red wine, and bay leaves. Turn to coat, then cover and marinate for 3 hours at room temperature or overnight in the refrigerator.
2 Light the barbecue or preheat a gas barbecue.
3 Thread the meat and the bay leaves onto skewers, alternating with onion and green pepper wedges.
4 Cook over hot coals, turning occasionally. Allow about 5–7 minutes for rare, 9–10 minutes for medium-rare, and 12–13 for well done. Serve at once.

82 TUSCAN-STYLE BEEF STEAK

Serves 4 as a main course

Ingredients

4 tender beef steaks, such as fillet or sirloin, 250g (8oz) each
3–4 tbsp olive oil
pinch of dried sage or oregano
salt and black pepper
juice of 2 lemons

1 Place the steaks in a shallow dish and pour over half the olive oil. Turn to coat, then sprinkle with the dried sage or oregano. Cover the beef steaks and leave to marinate at room temperature for up to 3 hours.
2 Light the barbecue or preheat a gas barbecue.
3 Grill the steaks over hot coals for about 8–10 minutes, or to taste (*Tip 74*), turning once.
4 Remove the steaks from the grill, season, then drizzle with the remaining olive oil and lemon juice to taste. Serve immediately.

83 THAI-INSPIRED PORK

Serves 4 as a main course

Ingredients

750g (1½lb) lean pork,
such as tenderloin, cut into
thin medallions
125ml (4fl oz) sherry,
port, or rice wine
125ml (4fl oz) chicken
stock
2 tbsp brown sugar
2–3 tbsp lime juice
Thai Spice Paste
2 tbsp grated ginger root
2 tbsp medium sherry,
port, or rice wine
60g (2oz) roasted peanuts,
coarsely chopped or
crushed
4 spring onions,
thinly sliced
1 tbsp vegetable oil
1 tbsp sesame oil
1 green or red chilli,
finely chopped
1½ tsp turmeric
1 tbsp brown sugar
1 tbsp balsamic or
raspberry vinegar
2 tsp ground cumin
1 medium bunch fresh
coriander, chopped
salt, to taste
black pepper

1 Blend the Thai spice paste ingredients together (since the nuts are salty, you may not need any extra salt, depending on taste).
2 Rub about half the spicy paste over the pork medallions, and leave for 1–3 hours at room temperature or overnight in the refrigerator.
3 Remove the meat from the paste with a slotted spoon, then place any mixture left behind in a saucepan with the sherry, chicken stock, sugar, and half the lime juice. Bring to the boil, then reduce the heat, and cook to form an almost syrupy glaze.
4 Light the barbecue or preheat a gas barbecue.
5 Cook the pork over hot coals until charred on each side but juicy inside. (Medallions are thin, so this will take only 2–3 minutes on each side.)
6 To serve, add the second half of the spice paste to the glaze (*Step 3*), together with the last 1½ tbsp of lime juice. Warm this sauce through, and put a spoonful or two on each plate with the pork.

LEAFY RICE GARNISH
Finely slice some red chillies and spring onion tops and mix with freshly cooked long-grain white rice. Fold four fresh banana leaves into a cone shape, securing with wooden cocktail sticks. Place each on a plate and fill with the rice mixture as a garnish.

BUTTERS, SAUCES, & SIDE DISHES

84 FLAVOURING BUTTER

Butter, flavoured with a variety of herbs and spices, makes a tasty accompaniment to barbecued foods. Simply serve a slice or two of butter on top of meat, fish, or vegetables straight from the barbecue, and leave it to melt, before eating. Alternatively, place a slice of flavoured butter inside a hamburger before cooking, and it will baste the meat as it barbecues.

▽ BARBECUED SALMON STEAKS
A nugget of chive, lemon, and watercress butter on top of each grilled salmon steak (Tip 62) enhances its flavour.

Unwrap and slice the chilled roll of butter

85 HOW LONG WILL BUTTERS KEEP?

Flavoured butters can be made well in advance of a barbecue. Unlike marinades and pastes, which tend to keep for only 2–3 days at most in the refrigerator, butters will keep for up to 1 week when chilled. Flavoured butters can also be frozen successfully and will keep for up to 2 months in the freezer. Before freezing, first seal the freshly made butter in clingfilm or wrap it up tightly in greaseproof paper. Allow the butter to defrost slowly at a cool room temperature for at least 2 hours before use.

86 ROSEMARY-MUSTARD BUTTER

For 1kg (2lb) lamb, chicken, or sliced potatoes

Ingredients

125g (4oz) unsalted butter, softened
1 tbsp French mustard
2 garlic cloves, finely chopped
2 tbsp chopped fresh rosemary
salt and black pepper

With a fork, combine the softened butter with the French mustard, garlic, and rosemary, and season to taste.

87 BLACK OLIVE & SAGE BUTTER

For 1kg (2lb) turkey or hamburgers

Ingredients

125g (4oz) unsalted butter, softened
8–10 fresh sage leaves, chopped
2–3 tbsp black olives in oil, drained,
pitted (if necessary),
and coarsely chopped
2 garlic cloves, finely chopped
salt and black pepper

With a fork, combine the softened butter with the sage, black olives, garlic, and seasoning. Serve right away or chill.

88 SUNDRIED TOMATO & BASIL BUTTER

For 1kg (2lb) chicken breast, swordfish, or salmon

Ingredients

125g (4oz) unsalted butter, softened
4 garlic cloves, finely chopped
5–8 sundried tomatoes packed in oil,
drained, patted dry to remove
excess oil, and finely diced,
plus ½ tsp of the oil
3 tbsp finely chopped fresh basil leaves
salt and black pepper

Blend the butter, garlic, and sundried tomatoes. Work in the oil and chopped basil, then blend in some salt and pepper, to taste.

89 SHALLOT BUTTER

For 500g (1lb) fillet steak, prawns, or scallops

Ingredients

125g (4oz) unsalted butter, softened
dash of lemon juice
2 shallots, finely chopped
salt and black pepper

With a fork, combine the softened butter, lemon juice, and season with salt and pepper to taste. Serve at room temperature or chill and cut up into slices.

90 CORIANDER & CHILLI BUTTER

For 750g (1½lb) prawns

Ingredients

125g (4oz) unsalted butter, softened
15g (½oz) chopped fresh coriander
3 spring onions, thinly sliced
2 garlic cloves, finely chopped
¼ green chilli, or to taste, finely chopped
dash of lime juice
pinch of grated lime zest
salt, to taste

Blend together the softened butter with the coriander, spring onions, garlic, chilli, lime juice, and lime zest. Season to taste with salt. Use at once, or wrap and refrigerate or freeze (*Tip 85*).

91 INDONESIAN PEANUT SAUCE

Serve with Chicken wings (*Tip 68*)

Ingredients

4 garlic cloves, finely chopped
2 tsp chopped ginger root
150g (5oz) crunchy peanut butter
2 tbsp sugar
4 tbsp water
Tabasco or other hot sauce, to taste
1 tbsp lemon juice
2 tbsp soy sauce
3 tbsp chopped fresh coriander
1 tbsp sesame oil
salt and black pepper

1 Mix the garlic with the ginger, peanut butter, and sugar.
2 Slowly stir in the water, then when emulsified add the Tabasco, lemon juice, soy sauce, coriander, and sesame oil. Season to taste.

92 MOJO ROJO

Serve with Monkfish kebabs (*Tip 61*)

Ingredients
1 medium-hot dried red chilli,
such as cascabel or arbol
1 tsp cumin seeds
125ml (4fl oz) water
5–6 garlic cloves, finely chopped
2 tbsp paprika
125ml (4fl oz) olive oil
2 tbsp red wine vinegar
salt, to taste

1 Bring the chilli, cumin seeds, and water to the boil and cook over a high heat for about 5 minutes.
2 Purée the garlic, add the chilli mixture and paprika, then slowly blend in the olive oil. Add the red wine vinegar and salt, and serve.

93 RED CHILLI AÏOLI

For 1kg (2lb) chicken, prawns, aubergines, or courgettes

Ingredients
100g (3½oz) prepared good
quality mayonnaise
1 garlic clove, finely chopped
1 tbsp mild red chilli powder
or pure mild chilli powder
1 tbsp paprika
¼ tsp ground cumin
1 tbsp chopped fresh coriander
dash of lemon or lime juice
2–3 tbsp olive oil
salt and black pepper

1 Combine the mayonnaise with the garlic, chilli powder, paprika, cumin, coriander, and a dash of lemon or lime juice.
2 With a whisk or fork, slowly blend in the olive oil, a little at a time, until it is absorbed. Season to taste. Chill the aïoli until ready to serve.

94 CUCUMBER-YOGHURT RAITA

Serve with Chicken tikka kebabs (*Tip 71*)

Ingredients

250g (8oz) natural thick yoghurt
½ cucumber, finely diced
2–3 garlic cloves, finely chopped
2 tbsp chopped fresh coriander or parsley
2 tsp chopped fresh mint, plus a few
sprigs to garnish
salt, to taste
pinch of cayenne pepper (optional)

Using a fork, blend all the ingredients together in a bowl and keep chilled until ready to serve. Sprinkle with cayenne pepper and garnish with fresh mint sprigs.

95 SHE-DEVIL BARBECUE SAUCE

Serve with All-American ribs (*Tip 75*)

Ingredients

1 onion, coarsely grated
3–5 garlic cloves,
finely chopped
4 tbsp Worcestershire
sauce
250g (8oz) tomato ketchup
4 tbsp molasses sugar
2–3 chipotle chillies
275ml (9fl oz) beer, plus
extra if needed
250ml (8fl oz) water, plus
extra if needed
1 tsp dry English mustard
powder
1 tsp mild red
chilli powder
1 tsp ground cumin
salt and black pepper
4 tbsp cider vinegar

1 Combine the onion, garlic, Worcestershire sauce, ketchup, molasses sugar, chipotle chillies, beer, water, mustard, chilli powder, cumin, salt and pepper, and half the vinegar in a large non-reactive saucepan.

2 Bring to the boil, then reduce the heat and simmer for 30–45 minutes, or until it forms a thick sticky sauce. If the mixture starts to burn on the pan base, add more water or beer.

3 Add the remaining cider vinegar to the sauce, and taste for seasoning. Remove from the heat.

4 When the ribs are nearly finished cooking on the grill, brush them with the barbecue sauce. Put the rest of the sauce in a bowl to dip into while eating.

96 THAI DIPPING SAUCE

Serve with meat, poultry, fish, or vegetables

Ingredients

*200g (7oz) chopped canned tomatoes,
with their juice*
2 tbsp dark brown sugar, or to taste
125g (4oz) sultanas, coarsely chopped
4 garlic cloves, finely chopped
½–1 dried red chilli, crumbled
½ tsp cayenne pepper, or to taste
*3 tbsp cider (or raspberry)
vinegar, or to taste*
salt, to taste
3 tbsp water, plus extra if needed

1 Combine the tomatoes with the brown sugar, sultanas, garlic, chilli, cayenne pepper, vinegar, and salt. Blend until the mixture is slightly chunky, adding water as necessary until the sauce has a slightly liquid consistency.
2 Pour the sauce into a pan and bring to the boil for a few minutes to allow the flavours to mingle.
3 When cool, add more vinegar, cayenne, salt, and sugar, to taste.

97 GUACAMOLE

Serve with Fajitas (*Tip 80*)

Ingredients

2 ripe avocados
½ onion, finely chopped
2 garlic cloves, finely chopped
2–3 tomatoes, diced
*½ fresh green chilli, such as jalapeño
or serrano, finely chopped*
juice of 1–2 limes
¼ tsp ground cumin
salt and cayenne pepper, to taste

1 Cut the avocados in half and remove the stones. Scoop out the flesh and mash coarsely.
2 Combine the avocado with all the remaining ingredients. Serve immediately, or cover tightly with cling-film to prevent air from turning the avocados black. Chill, and mix again well before serving.

98 SALSA
Serve with Fajitas (*Tip 80*)

Ingredients
3–5 garlic cloves, finely chopped
1 small onion, chopped
1 tbsp chopped fresh parsley
1 tbsp chopped fresh coriander
10 ripe tomatoes, skinned and chopped
1 tsp ground cumin
1–2 jalapeño or serrano chillies, finely chopped
1 tbsp lemon juice or vinegar
salt, to taste

Combine the ingredients with a fork. Purée if you prefer a smooth salsa.

99 REFRIED BEANS
Serve with Fajitas (*Tip 80*)

Ingredients
400g (13oz) cooked pinto beans, plus about 125ml (4fl oz) of the cooking liquid
4 tbsp vegetable oil
1 onion, finely chopped
salt, to taste
¼ tsp ground cumin
large pinch of mild chilli powder
250g (8oz) grated cheese, such as mild Cheddar or Pecorino

1 Using a potato masher, carefully mash the cooked pinto beans into the cooking liquid, leaving about a third of the beans whole or partially whole, to make a chunky-textured purée.
2 Heat the oil in a large pan, add the chopped onion, and sauté until soft and translucent. Add salt to taste, sprinkle with the ground cumin and chilli powder, then add approximately 125ml (4fl oz) of the bean mixture.
3 Cook over a high heat until the bean mixture thickens and reduces in volume, then add more puréed beans, stirring and mashing as you cook.
4 When all the beans have been added to the pan and the mixture is a thick creamy purée, it is ready to serve.
5 Sprinkle the bean purée with the grated cheese and continue heating gently until the cheese melts. (Do this on the barbecue for an extra smoky scent.)

100 BLACK BEAN SALSA

Serve with Swordfish (*Tip 63*)

Ingredients

175g (6oz) canned black beans, drained
2–3 ripe tomatoes, diced
1 garlic clove, finely chopped
1 spring onion, finely chopped
1 red or green Thai or serrano chilli, finely chopped
1 tbsp lime juice
¼ tsp ground cumin, or to taste
1–2 tbsp chopped fresh coriander leaves
salt, to taste

Mix all the ingredients together in a bowl, season with salt to taste, and serve.

101 MIDDLE EASTERN SPICED PILAFF

Serve with Cumin roast lamb (*Tip 79*)

Ingredients

90g (3oz) almonds, whole or slivered
60g (2oz) butter
60g (2oz) thin spaghetti, broken up
2 onions, thinly sliced lengthways
½ tsp ground cinnamon
¼ tsp ground cumin
250g (8oz) long-grain rice
500ml (16fl oz) hot chicken stock
100g (3½oz) raisins

1 Sauté the almonds in 15g (½oz) of the butter until golden brown. Remove and reserve.
2 Add another 15g (½oz) butter to the pan and brown the spaghetti pieces. Remove and reserve.
3 Sauté the onions in another 15g (½oz) butter until soft and golden. Sprinkle with half the cinnamon and cumin. Remove and reserve.
4 Sauté the rice in the remaining butter for about 3–4 minutes. Add the stock, raisins, and remaining cinnamon and cumin. Cover and cook over a low heat until the rice is half done.

5 Add the spaghetti to the pan, cover, and cook until both the rice and spaghetti are al dente, about 10 minutes. Fork in the onions and top with the almonds.

INDEX

ACKNOWLEDGMENTS

Dorling Kindersley would like to thank Hilary Bird for
compiling the index, Richard Hammond for proofreading,
Robert Campbell and Mark Bracey for DTP assistance,
Emma Patmore for preparing food for special photography, and
The Barbecue Shop, Cobham, Surrey and Landmann Ltd. for props.

Photography
Special food photography by Clive Streeter, assisted by Amy Hearn.
Special barbecue photography by Matthew Ward.
All other photographs by Dave King, Diana Miller,
David Murray, and Roger Phillips.